Merseyside

Edited by Heather Killingray

YoungWriters
First published in Great Britain in 2007 by:
Young Writers
Remus House
Coltsfoot Drive
Peterborough
PE2 9JX
Telephone: 01733 890066
Website: www.youngwriters.co.uk

SB ISBN 978-1 84602 801 4

Foreword

This year, the Young Writers' *2007: A Poetry Odyssey* competition proudly presents a showcase of the best poetic talent selected from thousands of up-and-coming writers nationwide.

Young Writers was established in 1991 to promote the reading and writing of poetry within schools and to the young of today. Our books nurture and inspire confidence in the ability of young writers and provide a snapshot of poems written in schools and at home by budding poets of the future.

The thought, effort, imagination and hard work put into each poem impressed us all and the task of selecting poems was a difficult but nevertheless enjoyable experience.

We hope you are as pleased as we are with the final selection and that you and your family continue to be entertained with *2007: A Poetry Odyssey Merseyside* for many years to come.

Contents

The Poems

The Dream

You were standing so lonely watching me,
Thinking about what we used to be,
Savouring those last few moments together,
Knowing this love won't last forever.

Your arms were open, welcoming me,
This was where I longed to be,
You looked at me, so I looked at you,
We were happy and that was true.

I want this moment to keep living on,
Before it's too late and the time has gone,
I looked up to the stars that gleam.
And all this time it was only a dream.

Holly Cope (13)

I Wish I Were . . .

I wish I were a cricketer
And scored more runs than Tendulkar
I would use all my tricks
And hit fours and six.

I wish I could fly
Stay high up in the sky
Forget football and kick the moon
And feed on stars with a spoon.

I wish I were a peacemaker
I would erase poverty and pain
Banish all wars and reasons to kill
Punish criminals who fight for cheap thrills.

Sparsh Garg (12)
Birkenhead School

My Wishes

I wish I had infinite wishes.
I could get what I want,
And what I don't want.
I could do whatever I like,
And make a great big fright!

I could have lots of money.
I could buy loads of gadgets,
And make a home for all the bats.
I could end all poverty,
And help the needy.

I wish the world lived in imperturbability,
So there wouldn't be any iniquity.
People will be very happy,
And live in complete harmony.

Oh, I wish, I wish . . .

Ammar Ahmed (12)
Birkenhead School

I Wish

I wish to be a footballer,
and bring a team right up,
I wish to be a footballer,
and lift the World Cup,
I wish to be a footballer,
I could play in any role,
I wish to be a footballer,
and score every goal.

I wish to have a chocolate bar,
which never runs out,
And stuff my face all day long,
but I would be sure to get gout,
I wish to have a chocolate bar,
but I would get very fat,
I wish to have a chocolate bar,
I'll be greedier than a rat.

But most of all I wish to have a long and happy life,
and spend it with a really beautiful wife,
and have lots of kids, who play with toys,
and dance around and make a noise,
I would also like to be really rich,
and own my own football pitch.

Tom Williams (12)
Birkenhead School

The Island

I wish I could own my own island
That's just off the coast of Ireland
Where I will sit down
With a very big crown
And constantly say,
'This is my land!'

Shaun Wilbraham (12)
Birkenhead School

Three Wishes

I wish I could cook like Gary Rhodes,
And cook on a ship like the Mary Rose,
I'd cook for my friends and my family too,
While sailing on top of the deep blue.

I'd wish for a moneymaking machine,
So I could buy most things from my dreams,
I would give a lot to charity,
To help my thoughts have clarity.

My dad has not been very well,
I'd wish him better, so he could tell
Me when I'm being wrong or right,
So that my heart would soar up like a kite!

Matt Smith (12)
Birkenhead School

A Child's Wishes

I wish it was Christmas every day,
I wish Santa Claus was here to stay.
I wish my piggybank was so very full,
It looked less like a pig and more like a bull.
I wish I had a super car,
I could drive so fast and far.
I wish the teachers would listen to *me!*
If they don't they'd better flee.
Now my wishes have come true and I have it all,
I don't think life's so content or such a ball.
I now wish for the good old days,
When I would just sit and wish and gaze.

Andrew Johnston (12)
Birkenhead School

My Wish

(Dedicated to my nan who has just recovered from breast cancer)

I wish that I could cause the sun
to warm the world with love
remove the clouds, a moment
to reveal the stars above.

I wish that I could wipe that tear
from the corner of your eye
bring happiness for your sorrow
bring a smile for your sigh.

I wish that I could do better things
put hope within your heart
make today the best you've had
right from its very start.

I wish that I were able
to make your dream come true
I wish I could - I wish I could
do all these things for you.

Joshua Aaron Catterson (12)
Birkenhead School

Football Crazy

I'm football crazy!
I'm football mad!
In a way I feel just like my dad,
I'm football crazy!
I'm football mad!
It's just what my grandad used to say,
'Try playing football it's good pay,
When you're at Liverpool make sure you stay.'
It's football crazy!
It's football mad!
If you think I'm sad,
You'll have to live with that.

Allan Lowey (12)
Birkenhead School

I Wish

I wish I could help animals that get abused
So they can live without a bruise.

All the animals in the world.
Cats, dogs and cattle herd.

I also wish for world peace.
So we can live in harmony.

Impossible I hear you say,
But hopefully I'll find a way.

Starting now upon this day.
To become a vet may be my way.

Cherish what you hold so deer.
I hope my poem will endear.

Tom Beaumont (12)
Birkenhead School

The Wishes Of My Heart

I wish I knew everything
I could cure anything at all
diseases, problems, evil
even being small.

I wish for a million pounds
so I could buy a lot
and with my new found knowledge
it would never rot.

I wish to be the best chef
then I could be
very, very famous
for my pastrami.

James Moses (12)
Birkenhead School

I Wish

I wish to end all poverty
To help those in need
So children don't die every minute
And we don't have to grieve.

I wish for all the knowledge
To keep me from school
So I can enjoy my childhood
And not worry about being a fool.

I wish I never famish
I never want to parch
I just want some money
To have when times are hard.

David Boffey (12)
Birkenhead School

I Wish

I wish I had a money tree so I would never be poor.
I could buy whatever I wanted and more and more.
I could buy the world and everything in it.
There would be no poverty in my world.

I wish I could fly, so I could fly away into the clouds.
I could soar and swoop as free as a bird.
When I was bored I could fly away into my world.
I would never be bored in my world.

I wish there was no school, no lessons and no homework.
I could spend my time doing what I wanted, not stuck in class.
The thrill of sport not the drag of homework.
That would be the ultimate world.

Tom Dodds (12)
Birkenhead School

I Wish, I Wish

I wish, I wish that I had a wallet
Where you ask the amount, which it spits out of its gullet.

I also wish, I wish to know all the knowledge
So I don't have to end my life jumping off a ledge.

And last of all I wish I had elemental powers
So I could make sinners and the criminals of the world cower.

William Robinson (12)
Birkenhead School

My Wishes

Imagine, imagine my dreams were fulfilled,
To end all war, poverty and more.
Imagine, imagine if all this happened,
We could run around free filled with joy.

I wish, I wish to end all poverty,
It would be a novelty.
I wish, I wish to end this suffering
There would be a world of loving.

I dream, I dream to make everlasting ice cream
The taste so cold, it makes me feel bold.
If this comes true it would be my dream,
To make everlasting ice cream.

James Ralston (12)
Birkenhead School

Footie

The ball was coming closer, closer.
I steadied my feet and prepared myself.
The ball on my head always hurts, but if I
Played my cards right, I could win control.

I made contact with the ball and gained control.
The other players made their call.
I wasn't sure where to pass.
I made my decision and kicked it hard.

The ball came back at speed.
I wasn't sure what to do.
There were players on me and I made the long ball.
My pass was so good, it helped another player
Score, a cracking goal.

Jack Crane (13)
Birkenhead School

I Wish

I wish I was a wealthy boy,
With lots of cash to spend,
I could buy anything,
And my fun would never end.

If I could wish for anything,
To make my life complete,
I would wish for girls at Birkenhead,
Who would fall down at my feet.

If I could choose a final wish,
To make me feel at ease,
I would spend my life in perfect health,
Immune from all disease.

Adam Snee (12)
Birkenhead School

Silver-Rimmed Glasses

Chewing on the end of a cigarette,
Silently observing the beautiful people with their
Diamond, Dior and decadent lives.

I look like them, act like them.
However at the moment I am their bridesmaid.

Flick, flick.
Sigh.

I continue to watch from my window sanctuary
Beyond into Tiffany's,
Ah how I wish one of those diamond masterpieces
Would drape my neck or adorn my finger.

Flick, flick

Don't you worry, I'll be in that club soon,
Who can blame a girl for dreaming?
If we can't dream, we won't know what we truly want in life
Or who we are.

Stub.

Helen Johnson (17)
Carmel RC Sixth Form College

My Fabulous Cats

M y fabulous cats
Y awning as they lie on the couch

F antastically they leap edge to edge
A mazingly they battered the dog
B ravely he balanced on the net
U nfortunately he fell off and landed on the telly
L uckily he tried again and did it
O bserved their food getting put out
U nderneath the couch
S taring all around.

C rafty Puddles thinks he's a dog
A nd rolls around like a wild mutt
T winx thinks she's a cuddly toy
S he curls up on me and falls asleep.

Luke Ellis (11)
Chesterfield High School

Break Dancin'

Break dancin', a way of life that's what I say,
Doing it from the heart, every single day,
Doing a handstand,
On any piece of land.

Swanny was my old mentor,
And always made us do a little bit more,
But now his time has past,
Swanny's memory will always last.

Now the new guy Dave,
It would look funny if he was dancing in a cave,
A man who tries and tries,
And who certainly never lies.

And now we're shattered glass,
And now am on a task,
To get into broken glass,
That would be my break dancing mass.

'Ye only in school for a couple of years,
If ye want to dance, do it to your best,'
Slim Tim 'Broken Glass'.

Joshua Pierce (12)
Chesterfield High School

Best Friends

My best friend Faye, she is the best,
We have our up and down moments,
Her blonde hair and blue dazzling eyes,
She looks like a princess.
She loves to dance and sing,
My best friend Faye, she is the best.

My best friend Taz, she is the best,
We have hills and ditches,
Her strawberry-blonde hair and sparkling eyes,
She looks like a princess,
She loves to talk and pose
My best friend Taz, she is the best.

My best friend Kelly, she is the best,
We have our smiles and cries
Her dark brown hair and twinkling eyes
She looks like a princess,
She loves to shop and go out.

My best friends are here for me, I am here for them
My best friends are the best, better than the rest.
My best friends, I will never forget my three best friends.

Erin Booth (12)
Chesterfield High School

Grandad

Grandad please sleep peacefully,
And no there isn't any way,
That anyone could replace,
The love you brought each day.
You brought so much happiness,
And fulfilled many dreams,
For in every word you said,
And in all your caring deeds.
I'll remember all the joy you brought,
When upon you I will call,
As I relive all the memories,
Once again, my tears will fall.
I miss you very much,
And would gladly like to say,
That your love upon my life
Is around me every day.

Elizabeth Barrett (12)
Chesterfield High School

Sunshine

S unny sunset glows in the morning
U nder the light blue sky,
N ot wet or cold at early hours
S hiny orange-coloured ors
H eavenly silent sounds
I n the sky in the morning
N ever down at noon.
E very sound, smell or sight of a beautiful sunshine.

Bernice Sullivan (12)
Chesterfield High School

Desert Horses Gallop Wild And Free

Galloping down the great savannah,
The sunset is nearly gone.
One thousand horses wild and free,
Came thickly thundering on.

Their hooves stamp a timeless beat,
As the wind flows through their manes
Horses' silhouettes stand tall and proud
In sheer blackness of the African plains.

The moonlight shines on a newborn foal,
It gleams brightly up in the sky.
The mare licks her small, weak offspring,
As it tries to stand up by her side.

There are harsh, freezing climates,
In the heart of the African night.
The herd stay close together,
As they all begin to take flight.

The horses soar through the mist,
The sun arises again.
Magnificent savannah wildlife,
Awake from their dens.

Heads held up high and alert,
Tiny ears pricked up in delight.
Fresh hooves of foals will dance around,
On warm sand in the new daylight.

Becci Morris (12)
Chesterfield High School

The Girl Called May

One day there was someone called May
Who hated that day because her mate called Grace
Set her up on a date.
She thought her mate, Kate, knew who it was.
Her date wasn't her mate, it was Andrew
Who never knew till that day,
That he had a date with May.

Chloe McNeill (12)
Chesterfield High School

Hallowe'en Poem

H allowe'en is nearly here,
people shriek and jump in fear.
A ll the children dressed to scare,
a ghost, a witch, a vampire over there.
L ots of laughter in the street,
children doing trick or treat.
L oaded bags full of sweets,
enough to keep them going for weeks.
O nce a year, it's quite enough,
say the parents with a laugh.
W eird painted faces in the dark,
eggs and flour leave their mark.
E veryone lighting pumpkins, with candlelight,
that one gave me such a fright.
E xcited children enjoyed their fun,
Hallowe'en party's now just begun.
N ight has come to an end,
but Christmas is just around the bend.

Amelia Johnson (13)
Chesterfield High School

My Poem About School

I thought that school would be as simple as a cloud,
Until I realised the teachers could be very loud,
I realised in music there were lots of sounds,
And outside the railings were well out of bounds.

I thought that school would be very simple,
Until everyone came down with a load of pimples,
We used to spin a dice, which was a game of chance,
And in PE they even tried to make me dance.
I felt all weird, from the moment I entered,
I'm starting to wish school was never invented.

Some people say it's really cool,
To listen and learn and do well in school.
Keep your head down boy, and tune in your ears,
And don't muck around like some of your peers.

Those who work hard and give it their best,
Will find they do better than all the rest.
English, maths and sciences too,
Learning opens up a great world for you.

Richard Hollis (12)
Chesterfield High School

Ship, Sea And Destiny

The ocean waves,
Washed over me
As my beloved ship sank.

The galley was filled with water,
The crew had long since dispersed.
Abandoned, all on my own.

A storm was a-brewing,
As plain as can be,
My life was flashing before me.

When I was one, two and three,
When I first went to sea,
Oh, how had it come to this?

So this is the fate,
That I must await,
To sleep with the fishes at sea.

Adam Jones (12)
Chesterfield High School

Pudding

The puddings I like best are sweet,
not savoury ones all stuffed with meat.

Melting sauce of chocolate fudge cake
Roly-poly filled with jam
All floating on a custard lake.

I like the taste of apple pie
all crumbly, sweet and piled high.

Oh and of course I can't forget the many flavours,
of yummy ice cream
stuffed in a sundae with strawberry sauce and chocolate flakes,
must insist on those sprinkle shakes.

You may not know but you might have guessed,
I have a sweet tooth and it's puddings I love best!

Sophie Sands (13)
Chesterfield High School

The Drastic Storm

The storm was savage!
Raindrops smashing into everything in sight.
Hailstones felt like such a burning light.
I kept thinking what a destructive storm
I held onto her hand
Which felt fairly warm.
I couldn't remember anything from the past ghastly day,
But we're worried about another heavy storm to come next May!

Hannah Southwood (13)
Chesterfield High School

Flowers

Fuchsias can be pink,
Lilies I like white.
Orchids make me wink.
Waterlilies bob and float
Evening primroses help me think.
Roses can be red or blue.
Some flowers come from seeds.
Some flowers even are weeds.

Sophie Tucker (11)
Chesterfield High School

Questions!

Why did you do it?
What did I do?
I was your best mate,
Mine was you,
Someone said something.
Why did you listen to their blabber,
When you knew it wasn't true?
You ordered me here,
Pushed me there,
You made me worried and made me despair.
After what you did,
Everything you said,
You phoned me up,
I was in bed,
Mum gave me a message,
From the call you gave
And this was the message,
'Be my friend again.'

Jessica Saunders (12)
Chesterfield High School

My First Day At School

I remember my first day at school
Where all I did was copy out rules,
I remember being out on the playground
But running out of school, was outta' bounds,
I remember my first lesson
Where all I did was a lotta' messing
I remember going home
Where I was free and allowed to roam.
I remember the end of the night
Where I learnt to pick up a pen and write.

Andrew McBrion (13)
Chesterfield High School

Physical Educational School

I remember when I got detention
Like a prisoner in jail
Because I talk all the time
So hopefully this poem should rhyme

In my class of PE
I do football
When I hit the ball
It glides into the back of the net

In my class of English
I do 'Goodnight Mr Tom'
But I'm doing a poem
Which I find boring
So I go to sleep
And start snoring.

When I watch football
Seeing Wayne Rooney play
He sickens me cos he looks like Shrek
Now he's got me watching Star Trek!

Michael Hill (12)
Chesterfield High School

The Morning Lake

Children playing,
Birds flying,
Parents chatting,
Grandparents snoring,
As the sun shines on the lake,
The golden lake as children laugh
Splash and play!

Amy Williams (12)
Chesterfield High School

Friends!

Friends are the ones who are always there,
The ones who tell you to change your hair,
They make you laugh, they make you cry,
They're always there for you, until the day you die.
We've all had our ups, and we've all had our downs,
But forget about that, get rid of those frowns!
Yes, they're the ones who are with the fashion,
Well guess what? It's our favourite passion!
So friends are basically the absolute best,
And there's no doubt about it, because they're better than all the *rest!*

Alison Bold (12)
Chesterfield High School

Grandpa Don

Cradling my tiny head.
Only one day old.
I'm gurgling with delight,
He makes sure I don't get cold.

B&Q uniform.
A smile on his face
Amongst our family album
He never looked out of place

He made me laugh, when I cried
As loving as loving can be
He'd hold me close when a storm was blowing
And rock me to sleep

He was loved by everyone
But was a grouch at times
I loved him very much
Life's cruel but must go on.

Mollie Currie (12)
Chesterfield High School

My First Day

Walking down a long road,
Meeting friends,
Feeling excited,
Young,
Scared
Ding!
I had started,
Swarms of red,
Yellow,
Blue,
And green,
Other pupils squished us,
Blue blazers,
Books,
And a strange card,
The smell of sausage rolls,
As we stampeded like elephants,
Squished lockers,
New books,
The school is like a long maze,
Long and winding staircases,
Ding!
A sea of uniforms flushed out of school,
It was the end,
Of my first day.

Samuel Thompson (12)
De La Salle RC High School

My First Day

We all flooded into the hall,
Like the sea rushing onto the shore.
My heart was going
Thud,
Thud,
Thud.
We found out our forms,
And our form teachers.
I was nervous but I felt I was getting older.
My mind was confused,
With all these classes.
I went into the corridor,
It was swarming with blue.
The bell went for home time
'One day over,
Phew!'

Jodie Graves (11)
De La Salle RC High School

Tsunami - Where Are They?

Think back, can you?
Are they still here?
The colossal towering monster, gone,
Black evil hands of the Devil, gone,
Dracula's great cape of water, gone,
Those roaring waves that haunt your mind,
Your loving family, they fell behind,
Where are they?

While you wonder on your own,
Nothing is the same,
Screams of terror, some delight,
People find their families,
Dead, alive, people are always found, but,
Where are they?

Turn the corner blink, then start to cry,
Hundreds dead before you,
Yet movement amongst the huddle,
Your tiny sister! She needs a cuddle,
Elimination of a city so big,
Now reduced to nothing more than a twig,
And even in the small happiness found,
Your fear still hasn't sank to the ground,
Amongst the dead, you and sister in bliss,
But, can you still answer me this? Where are they? Where are they?
Many loved ones and families are gone,
Gone, gone, gone . . .

Jennifer Rigby (14)
De La Salle RC High School

First Day

As I stepped out of the car.
All you could hear were buses squeaking, people talking.
Entering the crowd of blue.
People pushing and shoving
Trying to get into . . .
De la Salle.

Feeling lost, I searched for my classrooms.
Finally I found my first lesson.
Teacher seems nice.
Will they stay like that?
Friendships occurring
As I enter
The De la Salle family.

Alison Ruck (11)
De La Salle RC High School

Cycling

If you want to cycle
just get on your bike
because I think this is something
you are going to like.

You must wear a helmet
remember safety first
and don't forget your water
because this will quench your thirst.

Some people ride for fun
some people like to race
some people like to exercise
just go at your own pace.

You don't need to cycle all the time
but it will keep you fit
swap McDonald's and TV
for a little bit.

So do you want to cycle?
Don't let it pass you by
exercise is so much fun
why not give it a try?

Victoria Graham (11)
De La Salle RC High School

My First De La Salle Day!

'Night, night'
September 4th 2006
On my bed
Cheerful, happy and excited.
Nervous.
Dark, black,
Glimpse of light.
Hours pass,
Time flies by
Will I miss it?
Will I not?
'Daniel, time for school.'
On comes the blazer,
I feel proud.
Quick, the bus!

'Welcome to De La Salle'
Lots of noise,
Seas of blue,
Lots of pupils.
Form 7H, Bardsey
Daniel Lee.
Off to our room, I've got Mr Cooper.
Anxious, nervous.
Mazes of corridors.
Information, A-Z, all I need,
Then comes lessons
Tech,
English,
PE.
Bing, bing
A bell.
Smiling, happy.
Off to the bus stop,
First day
Gone.

Daniel Lee (12)
De La Salle RC High School

My First Day

Driving in the car
The wheels are slowing down
Crack, crack, crack, the leaves around me
Giggling of friends
Nerves all building up
Immense and worrying
Too many people
Too many teachers
Family, friends' words in my head
And then it's time
There's no going back!

Daniel Allen (12)
De La Salle RC High School

A Gift To Lourdes

Hello Lord it's me again
all my prayers will never end
I have found strength in You
hopefully You have found it in me too

Looking out my window today
we said the rosary and began to pray
I guess this is what I'm trying to say
You have made me stronger today

Oh Lord I've got to go
there's just one thing You need to know
I will love You any way
any time and any day.

Samantha Thompson (13)
De La Salle RC High School

If I Could Freeze Time

If I could freeze time,
I would freeze it here.
Where I am meant to be,
Safe in your arms.
For you hold our love as tight
For you know you are Mr Right.
When you are sad
I will push away the tears
When you are scared
I will fight away your fears.
When you need my love
You will have my heart
You help me through life
The kindness in your smile
The magic of your touch
These are the reasons I love you so much.

Grace Mooney (15)
De La Salle RC High School

Autumn

Crumbling leaves in the wind,
People shouting, jumping around:
Gusts of coldness in and out,
Drafts creep in, quiet as a mouse,
Children climbing up the trees,
Throwing acorns at their enemies.
When people go to bed, a certain bird comes out,
The owl's eyes are wide and big,
Ready to catch its prey.
The wolf howls, the moon is out,
Ready for the night,
In the morning, leaves are falling from the trees,
Some brown, some red,
And when morning dawns,
It's all going to happen again!

Louise Naylor (11)
Fazakerley High School

Decorating My Room

One tin of paint, wet and runny
Brush it on red
Let's move ahead.
Two rolls of wallpaper
Two bags of paste
Put it on my wall now
My room will be ahead.
Three bags of nails
Up goes my wardrobe
And on goes my shelf
Four bags of wood floor
Glue it in, pin it in
Now my room looks great
Just put my TV in.

Anthony Wilson
Fazakerley High School

LFC

First get the players ready and train.
Add footballs, linesmen, fans and goals too
The match, that will begin.
In the 89th minute Steven Gerrard scores.
The team, the fans, the manager and coach scream and
Shout with joy.

Jack Wilding (11)
Fazakerley High School

Third World Poem

Softly children are crying, crying softly,
Slowly children are dying, dying slowly,
But no one will help them as they are too poor!
Their countries are ridden with diseases and war.

Slowly children are starving, starving slowly,
Softly the children lose hope, lose hope, softly.
They soon realise to give up on their dreams.
Wondering why people won't help, wondering what does this mean?

If only I could help them, if only, if only.
But on my own I am helpless, I am helpless, helpless.
With your help they can achieve,
Their hopes and their dreams,
But without, they will suffer, softly, slowly . . .

Jessica Heron (12)
Fazakerley High School

To Be Or Not To Be Human

To be human you don't have to be rich.
You don't have to be poor.
All you need is a heart.
And a soul.

To be human you don't have to be black or white.
English or Pakistani.
All you need is a heart.
And a soul.

To be human you don't have to be old or young.
Male or female.

All you need is a heart.
And a soul.

To be human is not to be a Scouser
Not to be a Mank
All you need is a heart.
And a soul.

To be human you don't have to be a cricket fan.
Or a football fan.
All you need is a heart.
And a soul.

Jon Casey (11)
Fazakerley High School

Liverpool Football Club

We are the
We are the team!
We are the rest!
We are the best!
We can beat the
Best team in the world!
We can win the cup!
We watch!
We win!

Sarah Ormesher (7)
Fazakerley High School

My Own Football Match

First put in a stadium.
Then throw in some money.
Then add in some players.
Then immediately put in thousands of people in a crowd
Stir a ball and goal in,
Not too close now, they might *score!*
Add some refs
Then finally put in two changing rooms.

Amy Moses (11)
Fazakerley High School

Sunflower, Sunflower

Sunflower, sunflower dancing in the air.
Swerving, swerving around everywhere.
Looks like the sun yellow and bright
Growing taller and taller over the night.
Smells like perfume, it's ever so nice
Leaving the aroma smell over the light.
But here comes a rain cloud
It covers the sun.
No brightness, no light, no sparkle at all.
More rain clouds come together
They join making rain heavier and heavier.
It's coming down quick, lashing down
Even drowning the animal's flowers and bugs.
Suddenly stops, leaving everything dead
No sparkle, no brightness, all just wet.
Leaving the sunflower lying in its flower bed
Lying dead in the light, all dented with fright.

Nicole Williams (11)
Fazakerley High School

Animals Go Wild

I can run like the wind
I can smell what humans can't
I can hear low sounds
I love being a dog

I can run like a cheetah
I can pounce like a fox
I can creep like a quiet mouse
Don't be scared I'm only a cat

I can dive like the wind
I can dart through the sea
I love to play with people
I'm only a nice dolphin

I can run like the wind
I can pounce the best
I can sometimes be friendly
I'm only a cute cheetah.

Sophie O'Connell (11)
Fazakerley High School

I Love Music

The twang of guitars
The bounce of drums
The clash of the bands
The rhythm of dance
The rhyme of violin
The cello is the same
The piano keys twing
The perfect of the song
The happy people clap
The band has five saps
The banjo sound
The keyboard keys
I love music.
Hey! Yeah!

Terry O'Ncill (11)
Fazakerley High School

Green

Green is an Irish leprechaun, the best hide-and-seek player
of them all.
Green is the new, lush grass being eaten by the newborn lambs.
Green is the sloppy seaweed sitting on the wet sand.
Green is the football team running out on the pitch for the Cup Final.
Green is the yucky and horrible sprouts in our school dinners.
Green is the stem, the backbone of a plant.
Green is the Christmas tree with all its decorations and shiny lights.
Green is the shiny birthday paper, waiting for the little boy
to rip it apart.

Green is *everywhere!*

Daniel Moorcroft (11)
Fazakerley High School

Red

Red is love.
Red is the colour of a Ferrari.
Red is the colour of my room.
Red is danger.
Red is my favourite colour.
Red is for Liverpool.
Red is the colour of the morning sky.
Red is blood.
Red is the sunset.

Liam Harding (11)
Fazakerley High School

The Boat Trip

A tree whistles far ahead,
As a cavalry of foaming waves rush to shore,
The boat rocks, as the sea life below pulls us towards an island of paradise.

But the boat pulls up at the harbour,
Dolphins leap begging us to see their home,
An undersea world of happiness.

Jessica McGhee (11)
Fazakerley High School

The Alien Poem

The alien is as green as a football kit.
The alien is as dumb as an animal.
The alien is as spotty as a goblin.
The alien is as ugly as a lion.
The alien is as slow as a bike.
The alien is as horrible as a lion.

The alien has a big head, like the top of the rocket.

Matthew Hunter (11)
Fazakerley High School

The Alien

It came from space and landed on the Earth
In Bethlehem it looked like a Smurf
It went to London and it looked much worse
But it still looked better than Captain Kirk
It went to America and it just fitted in
It was the happiest it had ever been
It went to Korea and it got shot in the head
With a nuclear missile, it ended up dead.

Luke Neal (11)
Fazakerley High School

Liverpool

L iverpool is fun and joy.
I t is irresistible.
V ery packed because it's so good.
E veryone is a scouser.
R eady for 2008.
P eople say it just makes you late.
O ver the time it has got better
O n the top of the Liver building there are two Liverbirds.
L iverpool is my favourite place.

Liam Moses (12)
Fazakerley High School

Three O'Clock

On Saturday and Sunday three o'clock never comes
You wait and wait and it never comes.
On Monday to Friday it comes like a flash.
When it comes we are all mad.
I wait for Tuesday I wait for three o'clock
Because then I do dance with all my friends.
Then we have some snacks like drinks and food.
I wait and wait for Friday to come back
Because it's the end of the week
And we have French where we don't know all
Different things about France.
Then at the end of school
We all go out with our friends
Till the start of the week comes *again.*

Natasha Hughes (11)
Fazakerley High School

Blue

Blue is a raindrop
Blue is a blueberry
Blue is a sea
Blue is sad
Blue is the sky
Blue is Everton
Blue is the water
Blue is a river
Blue is the colour of my pen
Blue is the colour of fish.

Connor Mclean (11)
Fazakerley High School

The Teddy Bear Star

I have a special friend
His name is Teddy Bear
He lives as a shining star
But don't ask me how he got there.

There in his eyes
Is a certain glitter
The one thing he isn't
It is bitter.

My best friend
Honest he is a star
But we have a special friendship
Because we live so far.

I sigh and say goodbye
But then I see his smile
And our friendship
It seems more worthwhile

So I wave goodbye
And blow a kiss
My special friend
I'm going to miss.

Antonia Ferguson (12)
Fazakerley High School

Liverpool

They never walk alone
But they just walk and they do not stop
Until they get to the six yard box
And they keep on singing until they have stopped singing.
They have scored a fantastic goal by Steven Gerrard
And they have been shouting, 'Goal, goal, goal,
Goal, goal, goal.'

Ryan McKay (11)
Fazakerley High School

Nature

As I walked through the park,
I saw a million hands waving at me
'It was only the trees getting blown by the wind'

Looking up, down,
There's wildlife everywhere
They remind me of little balls of energy
Bouncing around
'It was only a little squirrel'

Strolling through the magnificent field
Covered in confetti scattered at a wedding
'It was only some flowers'

On my way home from the park
The sun shone, the rain fell,
Lightning struck and snow gracefully twirled,
Leaped and fluttered to the ground
'It was only my imagination.'

Chloe Bennett (11)
Fazakerley High School

Why?

Why don't you answer the phone Ashleigh?
Why did you choose a different school?
Why won't you talk to me Ashleigh?
Why do you think I'm uncool?

Don't you like me Ashleigh?
I bet you would kill me if you could.
Would you put a gun to my head?
Sometimes do you think that you should?

Why are you saying things about me Ashleigh?
Things that aren't even true.
Why are you spreading rumours Ashleigh?
Is it just something else to do?

What do you want from me Ashleigh?
Whatever happened to you?
Now you really hate me.
And why? I haven't got a clue.

I think I'll leave you alone now Ashleigh.
I won't bother you anymore.
I'll pretend I'd never met you.
I'll stop knocking at your door.

Did I just lose my best friend?
But I think I'll be OK.
But actually to be honest, I didn't like her anyway.

Charlotte Dunne (11)
Fazakerley High School

The Cricket Team

The team marched onto the pitch
With the VIPs that were picked
The crowd got their seats
And stomp went their feet!
So the game had begun.
The spin bowler bowled
And the batter hit and ran
The ball was in the air
The fielder leaped
Without a peep
Because he didn't care
It was caught with one hand,
On demand
And then the fielder landed
The crowd went wild and they
Smiled and that was the game.
But in that game there was no dame
Like the jousting history game.

Scott Craven (11)
Fazakerley High School

My Class

We are as naughty as hyenas.
We are as funny as chimps.
We are as noisy as elephants on drums.
We are as lively as cheetahs.
We are as clever as parrots.

Lee Holyland (11)
Fazakerley High School

The Poltergeist

I see a house of ghouls
As far as I can see
If you go in there you're fools
Even you and me.

I go to the scary house,
I see a shadow that is black,
I see a ratty mouse,
And I get tingles down my back.

I open the creepy door,
I see a small trace,
I walk on a bit more,
Then I see a frightening face.

I see the scary ghost,
Flying up and down,
But what scared me the most,
Was him munching on a clown.

I am standing still, right here,
It flies towards me now,
I am frozen in fear
As it spits out the bones of a cow.

There it goes,
With its big sharp teeth.
Nobody knows,
If it was the ghost chief.

Now I am dead,
In this warehouse there is a crack,
I will chop off your head,
That's when my spirit is coming back.

Curtis Hepplestall (11)
Fazakerley High School

To Be Or Not To Be Human

To be human is to work your hardest,
Not to be human is to slouch and yawn.
To be human is to care for animals,
Not to be human is to train them to kill.

To be human is to express yourself,
Not to be human is to keep it all inside.
To be human is to tell the truth,
Not to be human is to lie all the time.

To be human is to do as you're told,
Not to be human is to rant and rave.
To be human is to have confidence,
Not to be human is to be shy and quiet.

To be human is to do your work,
Not to be human is to write nothing.
To be human is to save the rainforest,
Not to be human is to kill the trees.

Toni Bates (11)
Fazakerley High School

Why Mum, Why?

Why don't you put the bin out Mum?
Why has Dad got a big bum Mum?
Why don't you cook Mum?
Why would you like my room clean Mum?
Why do you think Nan is so mean Mum?
Why can't I play in the mud Mum?
Why do you like me clean Mum?
Why can't I run wild in the kitchen Mum?
Why don't you win the lottery Mum?
Why do you drive an old banger Mum?
Why don't you answer my questions Mum?
Why Mum, why?
Why don't we have a computer Mum?
Why do we have to go to school Mum?
Why does my brother play pool?
Why Mum, why?

James Windsor (11)
Fazakerley High School

Red

Red is blood
Red is anger
Red is Liverpool
Red is cherries
Red is a clown's nose
Red is on the England flag
Red is fury
Red is the Devil
Red is hot.

Stephen Regan (11)
Fazakerley High School

The Tsunami

Why does an Earthquake start a giant wave?
Why do things happen, where people can't be saved?
Storms on the seas and flash floods rising,
Earthquakes, bomb shakes, all surprising.

A colossal tsunami waiting to hit the land,
Rushing forward, then engulfing the sand.
People are screaming and trying to flee,
But who can escape a sonic wall of sea?

As it hits the shore and floods the town,
People, animals and the ground will drown.
The sound of crying from civilians dying
Will never win, but still are trying.

Once all is done and the sea is calm,
All is complete, goodbye fear and harm.
As no one is left except the lucky,
All hands and feet become so mucky.

Why do things happen, where people cannot be saved?
Just like the Earthquake and the giant wave.

Dylan Fox (12)
Fazakerley High School

Spirits

All of these happy souls
Who of which they passed
All have gone to a happy place
Where there is no better place.

There is no fighting, no hunting
Just those people who want to live again
Who are very happy because
Heaven is the place where they belong.

All the people down on Earth
Say a prayer for all the family
Who are in Heaven.

Kiera Daley (11)
Fazakerley High School

The Shipwreck

The lightning was striking,
It was absolutely frightening.
The waves were crashing and bashing
As the ship drove through the sea.

The moon was out and it was very dark.
I heard my dog bark,
It sounded like he was in pain,
And to him it was no game,
And it wasn't to me either.

Then I saw a light,
The light was very bright,
It was the only thing in my sight,
So I was very determined to get to it.

I didn't quite get there,
But as long as I had my friend Clare.
The sun came out and smiled at me,
I could finally go home,
Where I wouldn't be alone,
And I could tell everyone about the journey of me!

Megan Buckland (11)
Fazakerley High School

Why?

Why are people different, Mum?
Why are some people old?
Why are some people young, Mum?
Why do old people grow mould?

Why are some people black, Mum?
Why are some people white?
Why are some people good, Mum?
Why do some people fight?

Why do people smoke, Mum?
Why, even though they can die?
Why do people get fat, Mum?
Why do they live a lie?

Why is the war going on, Mum?
Why does it never stop?
Why does it happen in poor countries, Mum?
Why does a bomb go tick, tick, tock?
Why don't they ever learn, Mum?
Why? Why? Why?

Amy Herrera-Leon (11)
Fazakerley High School

Football

When you shoot and the keeper saves,
None of the crowd does Mexican waves.
When you're running and the defender slides,
Both of your legs fastly collide.

At half-time you have a break,
Sit down and have a protein shake.
When you pass the ball,
You hear the ref call . . . *'Offside.'*

Michael O'Keefe (11)
Fazakerley High School

I Think . . .

What's happening to our world?
I think . . .
With bombings here,
With fighting there,
I feel like nobody really cares!

What's happening to our animals?
I think . . .
Wild bears being trapped,
Baby seals being culled,
Most primates becoming extinct!

What's happening to our community?
I think . . .
Drug taking here,
Binge drinking there,
Where are the people that are supposed to care?

What about the elderly?
I think . . .
Some fought in World War I
Most also in World War II
Some people don't care, but I most certainly do!

What is there I can do?
I think . . .
I can't stop the wars,
I can't help all animals,
I can't save the world
Or could I? I wonder!

Emma Caunce (13)
Greenbank High School

Autumn

Autumn leaves are falling
Winter's drawing near
The days are getting shorter
At this time of year.

The air is getting colder
Better wrap up tight
Hats and gloves and scarves on
If you must go out at night.

Shelley Mackay (11)
Greenbank High School

Wishing

The girl wished
Wished for what?
The selfish things she wished for, money, clothes, mobiles
Then she realised that people in other countries
Didn't have that kind of money
She wasn't a selfish girl anymore
She was a kind and considerate girl
She had changed.

Katie Campbell (11)
Greenbank High School

Hallowe'en

All Hallow's Eve or Hallowe'en,
A walking nightmare, not a dream,
It's scary stuff, it's creepy too,
I'd stay indoors if I were you!

One night a year, belongs to those,
Whose evil dispositions pose,
In guises evil, weird and grim,
Stay indoors, I say, don't let them in.

Prepare your pumpkin lanterns,
Keep your homes light,
Be prepared, for I can't tell you what evil
Lies in store tonight.

Emily Clegg (11)
Greenbank High School

Bad News

(In memory of Auntie Margret)

We had some bad news,
When I answered the phone,
Nana had been crying and
Asked for Mum.

I was surprised when I heard the news
Auntie Margret had died,
I stood and watched Mum as she cried,
I gave her a hug.

I remember Auntie Margret
She was happy and smiley
She was always kind
And very funny.

She always loved dogs, she had two.
We played in the garden
Throwing them balls,
But they always came back to her calls.

I will miss her and I'm very sad
That she died.

Hope Deary (12)
Greenbank High School

Monster

I saw a monster in the woods today
As I was walking by,
I could hear the monster's footsteps going through the leaves
And making them crunch extremely loud,
His breath made everything crumble and die.

And when he raised his hairy arm
It blotted out the light and the sun;
He snatched a bird from the sky
And swallowed it down in one.

His mouth was like a dripping ocean,
His beady eyes like pools of lead,
And when he growled
I ran straight back home and rushed upstairs to bed.

That was yesterday and it's a new day
Although it gave me quite a big fright,
I'm older now and so much braver now,
So I'm going back tonight.

I will tie him up when he is in a deep sleep
And take him straight back to the zoo.
The trouble is he is rather big . . .
So will you help and come too?

Kayleigh Gilbert (11)
Greenbank High School

My Dog!

My dog will play
And eat and sleep
When we say, 'Walkies' he jumps up at your feet!

He has a little break in his tail
From when he was very small
When I touch it, it may still hurt
So I try not to touch it at all.

His tail sticks up
The wind in his hair
As we walk down Formby beach
With the strong salt smell, tearing through the air
His treats he tries to reach

He goes home sleepy
Tired and cold
Curling up in his basket
Without being told!

My little dog, sound asleep
In a land of all his own
His tiny mind filled with magical dreams
With a massive and juicy bone!

Olivia Moss (11)
Greenbank High School

Suffering Seven-Year-Old

Every day is like a chore,
And every night is like a war.
I still remember that night,
When something wasn't right
Blue and white lights surrounded me,
As everyone pointed miserably.

I was only seven years,
But still all them tears,
One little swerve,
And we hit the kerb,
You were all dead,
Or so they said.

To this day,
I think I should pay.
Because I left you in that car to die,
And didn't even say goodbye.
I wanted to get help so I got out of there,
But I stood there thinking where,
All I saw was that glare.

The car fell,
And that's the day I went to Hell.
People say it's fate,
But I say it's hate.
But I think I should be with you.

But I suppose I am still that seven-year-old,
Who stood up very bold.
And we are still together,
Forever.

I'm not blind,
I know it's in my mind.

Vicki Hannah (13)
Greenbank High School

Pawsha

I want to write a poem,
But I don't know where to start.
I think and think,
I wink and she winks.

She has big brown eyes,
And she sleeps beneath the skies.
She is very blonde,
And of whom I'm rather fond.

She is my best friend,
Our love shall never end.
She is my dog,
No, she is the only one who
Understands me better than myself.

With her dainty little paws,
People ask, 'Is she yours?'
She looks great in pink.
So who is she I think,
Well here's a start, her name is *Pawsha!*

Laura Willows (14)
Greenbank High School

Lost Girl

When it's cold outside,
And the rain pours down.
When you can't hear the thunder,
'Cause there's no one around.

Just look to the side,
And you'll see her there.
Cold and alone,
She sits on the stairs.

She's the little lost girl,
Surrounded by tears.
She cries all night,
But nobody hears.

She just wants someone to love her,
To keep her warm at night.
She lives in hope,
That one day, someone might.

Nicole Anderton (14)
Greenbank High School

The Feeling Of Dance!

Music makes me want to dance
It's a feeling that you can't control
It's like when I've been crying
And I'm empty and I'm full
But I don't know what it is
It's hard to tell
When I'm up there dancing, I can't stop
It's like I'm under a spell
The butterflies, the nerves, it's all worthwhile
When the audience applause, I just want to smile.

Frankie Armitage (13)
Greenbank High School

Why?

Why me?
Why do you hurt me?
Why do you make fun of me?
Why do you hate me?
Why me?

Why do you use me?
Pretending to be my friend
Why bully me?
Why bully anyone?
Why?

Why do you have to bully?
Why?
Why don't you like me?
Why is it because I am?
Weird? Different from you
Why?

Why o why?
Why do this?
Why hurt other people?
Why don't you be kind?
So why not be friends
Why this because what whatever goes around comes around?

Hannah Enell (13)
Greenbank High School

Without A Home

The curse of winter reaches out to me with tendrils of ice.
The peak of misery penetrates my thin, shabby coat,
Chilling me to the core.

And I wait for death, and it seems that
I embrace death; I welcome death, with open arms.

An end to my suffering,
An end to my pain.

I will die alone in these empty streets,

And litter shall be my shroud.

The curse of winter stretches out to me with daggers of frost.
The shadow of hopelessness penetrates my thin, shabby coat,
Freezing my very soul.

My misery seems complete,

Sitting on street corners in the rain,
Begging for money to pay for my addiction.
Four long years I have had a cardboard home.

If only I could have a job to pay for my demon.
If only I could stop.
But now I am addicted I cannot.

So I drag my feet through the lonely streets.

The curse of winter will kill me.

I will die alone in these empty streets,

And litter shall be my shroud.

Jaime Bolzern (12)
Greenbank High School

What Do I Believe In?

W hat happens when you die?
H eaven or Hell or a pit of nowhere?
A fterlife, what is it?
T he final journey that you ever take.

D o other people believe in what I believe in?
O pinions, people have many.

I s what I believe in right?

B eing the best you can
E njoying life to the full
L iving is believing to me
I ndependent is what you are
E verlasting memories live on in others
V alue, we are all the same
E nd to life is a big adventure

I s this right?
N ever to know till the time comes
?

Ashleigh Houston (14)
Greenbank High School

Smile

A smile is something that brightens your day,
Something that warms your heart.

A smile is something to show your love,
For someone who's special to you.

A smile is something that says you're happy,
When somebody makes you laugh.

A smile is something that everyone has,
That shines upon your face.

A smile a day, keeps the sadness away,
So keep the smile on your face!

Kirsty Flynn (12)
Greenbank High School

Desperation

I want to write a story
But know not what to say
How do I explain how my life got
Thrown away?

How I curled into the corner
Crying with pain and fear
How Mother never said hello
Goodnight my dear.

But instead she'd shout and rave
And scare me half to death
I wish that I could have shut it out
I wished that I was dead.

Always there were evil words
That held us all in tears
Dad always protecting
Shutting out my fears.

I know now the cause
Of my childhood pain
A swifty glass of spirits
Left not much to gain.

Now I want you to decide
If you are the violent type
To think about the drinking
And not cause a fight.

Decide if your child will be with me,
Along the blue sky
Or will you stay calm and ready,
And never play with alcohol?
Love, Teddy.

Jenny Iveson (14)
Greenbank High School

Nightlife

When a sheet of night pulls over,
And the streetlights flicker on,
The neon signs awaken,
Another day has gone.

Taxis stop and let people out,
The bars have come alive,
Already people are out and about,
It's really no surprise.

The music beats right through you,
Disco lights like the sun,
This is no place for relaxing,
Because the nightlife has begun.

Vikki Hercules (14)
Hilbre High School Humanities College

The Football Match

We kicked the match off
Lots of time to play.
'Come on you Reds,' we cheered the players all the way.

We picked up the ball down the left-hand flank.
Ran all the way to the corner flag.
Crossed the ball in, for a shot on goal,
They got on the end of it, to score a goal.

The match came to an end,
And our batteries were flat,
All in a day's work, we won the match!

Lewis Johansen (13)
Hilbre High School Humanities College

The Match

We queued up for our ticket
Eventually we got in
We were all excited
We hoped our team would win.

They came out through the tunnel
All the fans let out a scream
We saw Steven Gerrard
Chatting to the team.

The referee blew the whistle
The ball flew round the sky
The players scrambled round the pitch
Bellamy's shot was high.

All the fans went crazy
They thought a goal was scored
They sang and then they chanted
All the children roared.

80 minutes were over
With just ten minutes to bet
When Riise had a shot
It went flying into the net.

Liverpool fans were dancing
The Chelsea fans were sad
The ref then blew the whistle
And Benitez was very glad.

Ben Watson (13)
Hilbre High School Humanities College

The Fire

The air in the kitchen
was smoky and hot,
the flames were flicking
my sister was asleep in her cot.

I could hear frightened voices
the siren was loud
they had so many choices
fire burning, what a crowd

I miss them I do
my sister, my brother
they should have made it too
my father, my mother

I was still alive,
and I survived,
as they all died
I cried on the drive.

Aimee Lydiate (13)
Hilbre High School Humanities College

Autumn

Autumn comes like a robin,
Silently, but you know she's here.

Foggy dampness, grass wet underfoot,
Tendrils of mist drape like a white sheet.

Burnished leaves, red, gold and yellow
Scattered on the moist ground.

Leaves crunch like the sound of breakfast cereal,
Condensation on my windows,
Dripping, droplet by droplet.

Autumn's end goes like a robin,
Silently, but you know she's gone.

Callum McDougall (13)
Hilbre High School Humanities College

Heads Or Tails?

Am I fighting a battle,
That is already lost?
Is my fate decided,
A coin already tossed?

And if this is indeed true,
Then why do some get such a raw deal?
And others have servants,
To prepare their every meal?

Does it really matter,
Which path I take?
Or will I end up where I'm meant to be,
Whatever choices I make?

Should I really care,
Who gets hurt and who doesn't?
Who would really mind,
If my 'couldn't' was a 'wouldn't'?

Can I really save the world,
With what I do and say?
And should I really bother,
When others CBA?

Why do those with everything,
Sit at home to grow obese?
When they could give instead of spend,
And help the suffering cease?

Are they fighting a battle,
That is already lost?
Is their fate decided,
A coin already tossed?

Katie Wright (13)
Hilbre High School Humanities College

How Come?

You said to me,
'I'll always be there,
I am your rock.
You can count on me,
When the wind whistles,
And the thunder thuds,
I'll always be there.'

You said to me,
'You're as soft as the sun,
Your hair is as golden as barley,
Your nature is as kind as ever
I'll always be there.'

'I'll always be there.'
Is that what you said to me?
Then how come you never come round anymore?
Then how come your smile has faded like curtains in the sunlight?
Then how come the silence is louder than the things
you used to say?
Then how come when I gaze into your eyes, it's like staring
into space?

You said to me,
But how come?
You said to me,
But how come?

Caroline Swift (13)
Hilbre High School Humanities College

Sharpe

Soldier of line
The 95th rifles
Each shot is fired
From the 95th rifles.

For the cannon
We're building a trench
In preparation
To bombard the French.

For every order
We obey
Another enemy
We stay.

For we are the best
In Wellington's troupe
With clean uniform
Guns and boots.

Soldier of line
The 95th rifles
Each shot is fine
From the 95th rifles.

Alex Lamb (13)
Hilbre High School Humanities College

The Sea, A Writhing Dragon

The sea is a writhing dragon,
though beautiful, a dangerous foe.
It claws the cliffs, it strokes the shores,
though magnificent, it forever roars.
It devours the land, it licks the shores,
though at night the roars no more.

Samuel Ashcroft (13)
Hilbre High School Humanities College

Biking

Biking is a super sport,
I do it quite a lot,
Downhill racing is the best,
But 4X is just not.

Flatland biking is so cool,
But BMXing does so rule.
I wish I could do all of these
But now it's over, I'm not so pleased.

Richard Addicott (13)
Hilbre High School Humanities College

I'm Scared

Bullies, they have put me in a world,
a world full of fear,
each corner I turn,
each room I enter . . . I'm scared.

They are always there
with the punches and kicks
the hurtful comments . . . I'm scared.

I don't want to dread the next day
I don't want to be scared of the lonely walk to school
but it's true . . . I'm scared.

Can't they leave me alone?
Leave me be? . . . no, I guess not
can I have my friends back?
Can I have back my smile? . . . no I guess not.

Why choose me . . . ? Why hurt me?
all you do is make me scared
you won . . . I'm scared.

I'm scared
I don't want to be
I'm scared
and always will be
I'm scared.

Abigail Forshaw (13)
Hilbre High School Humanities College

The Room

As I close this dingy door my feet slip on the grimy floor,
All the mess on the floor,
It looks like there's been a war,
As I travel on this quest, I see smelly socks and dirty vests,
This is an endurance test.
To finish I try my best
Then I always wonder why,
This slimy, grimy, smelly quest leads me to my bed,
Isn't my room the absolute best.

Christopher Sutcliffe (14)
Hilbre High School Humanities College

Society Bullies Become The Bullied

The boys laugh, the girls cry,
The society had begun,
The hierarchy of the classroom is nigh,
Sanity has been undone.

The battle raged on, 'Man down! Man down!'
Fair is foul, foul is fair, no time to crack a frown,
Not a gun fight, but a fun fight,
Well, not if you're able to see the light.

'Stop!' the teacher shouts,
No one listened, no doubt,
But still the screams and screams,
To get out of this would be a dream.

'Man down! Man down!' The battle has ended.
The time has come,
To stop the fun, to pack it in,
The battle never began.

They said it was a social war,
If you implore, to adore, this war,
They all sat there, in their clans,
Wishing it never began.

Robert Povall (13)
Hilbre High School Humanities College

One Person

One person can break your heart,
One person can make you cry,
One person that you loved,
Because they didn't love you.
One person can make you laugh,
One person can make you smile
One person that you adored,
But you knew there was only one person for them.
You would talk to them every day,
To make sure they were OK,
They would say, 'I'm fine,'
And then ask you the same.
All the time you wanted to say,
I love you and always will,
But something was stopping you,
And that was a shame,
You wanted to let go,
You wanted to say goodbye,
You wanted to hurt them,
But all you could do was cry.
So when you didn't see them,
Even though it was only one day,
You knew what you should have done,
And now you're dark inside.
You got over them,
And managed to let them go,
But somewhere in that black hole,
Was a huge soft spot for them, you refused to remove.
So when that person came back to you,
Everyone saw the change,
Now your love is no longer a secret,
You know you shouldn't have left it inside.

Katherine Starr (13)
Hilbre High School Humanities College

My Auntie Val

My auntie Val is my mum's best mate
She likes cakes cream
And wine by the crate
She is Irish and crazy,
Talks quite a lot
Loves to do housework
I think not!

Hannah Smith (14)
Hilbre High School Humanities College

The Dog

At the end of your bed he sleeps,
In a great big heap he lies,
Living there like a lazy lump.
For a walk you should take him three times a day,
Throw him a stick and he will fetch it for you,
Give him a bone and he will chew it until it has gone.

Daniel Edwards (14)
Hilbre High School Humanities College

Roland

Roland is an overweight cat,
He isn't big-boned, he's just fat!
His belly wobbles to and fro,
Watch him eat and watch him grow,
You'll hear him miaowing in the night,
Because he's got an appetite,
His cheesy smile and tiny feet,
Will totter down the midnight street,
He knows it's time to lose some weight,
Before it really is too late,
So Roland's signed up at the gym,
In the hope that he'll get slim,
So the ladies won't laugh at him,
And at his triple, triple chin,
He hopes that soon he'll be their dream,
But first he'll finish his bowl of cream.

Emily Monk (14)
Hilbre High School Humanities College

A Match I Went To See

A match I went to see
Liverpool Vs Chelsea
A very good match to see
It was for the charity shield
Gerrard led us onto the field
The referee blew the whistle
Chelsea took a fall
Liverpool stole the ball
The crowd let out a roar
Aurelio was hit in the jaw
The ref pulled out a red,
'It was a penalty,' everyone said
Kuyt stepped up to take a shot
The keeper didn't miss it by a lot
Goal! One-nil to the Reds
The Chelsea fans bow their heads
The referee blew his whistle
Liverpool took the steal
The celebrations began
I'm Liverpool's most loyal fan.

Jamie Howitt (14)
Hilbre High School Humanities College

Animals

Bunny rabbits cute and fluffy
Floppy ears big and stuffy.

Horses galloping along the field
Jumping bushes, hedges and wheels.

Lions look around and roar
They eat different animals like deer and boar.

Monkeys so cheeky, eating their bananas
Swinging about playing gymkhanas.

Cats prancing around
Scratching and chewing everything they have found

Birds are tweeting in the sky
Singing happily as the day goes by.

Little mice running free
Up and down a sycamore tree
Collecting acorns for all to see.

Sophie Wearing (12)
Hilbre High School Humanities College

My World

Here I am on my fluffy, pink cloud
Beautiful fairies sing aloud
As they flutter through the sky
Prince Charming rides by
The shopping centre calls my name
When you're there you feel like fame
Shoes and bags are the best
All for fun, I'm impressed
Everything I want for free
Tinkerbell advising me
Which outfit shall I wear?
We will search everywhere
Zap me an outfit to try on
Tink always makes things fun
Now for Tink to do my hair
When I get to the ball, the prince will stare
Now I'm ready, it's been fun
I'll be with the prince till kingdom come!

Ellie Smith (12)
Hilbre High School Humanities College

Teacher's Poem

Miss Fletcher is cool,
And works at Hilbre High School.
Miss Moon is definitely the best.
And Mr Devenport rocks the rest.
Miss Pearce teaches us dance
Mr Pritchard gives us a chance.
Miss Gaunt keeps us in.
And Mrs Rewey tells her stories.
But Miss Bidwell teaches us maths.
And Mr Anderson likes to have some laughs.
Miss Flynn discovers the past.
And Miss Hodson says how it goes, so fast.

Katie Leigh (12)
Hilbre High School Humanities College

Horses

Galloping, prancing, trotting freely,
Balanced jump, good girl Keely.
Horses all different colours
Black, brown, grey
And don't forget Bay.
Jumping poles magnificently,
They're trying to buck I can see.
In the field they're happy and free,
But in the stable I know I'd hate it to be me!
Apples, grass, horses love that.
Eating happily all day.
But free again in mid May.
Bathtime is hard,
When you're not in the yard,
They know what's happening,
They're not stupid.
They could prance around all day,
People do say.

Holly Bullock (12)
Hilbre High School Humanities College

If I Was A Pirate

If I was a pirate I would sail the Seven Seas,
I'd go and see the places, that I have always dreamed.
I'd go to France, I'll dance, all night until the break of dawn.
If I was a pirate, I would sail the Seven Seas.

One day I would meet this baddy, his name would be Big Fat Daddy.
We would fight all night, until the sun would come up high in the sky.
If I was a pirate, I would sail the Seven Seas.

My ship would be big, bright and bold and stand out in the dull sea
I would stand out on the front of the ship, to show that I was proud
My journey would finally come to an end, the dream would never last.
If I was a pirate I would sail the Seven Seas.

Ellie Newby (12)
Hilbre High School Humanities College

Music

M uffled music which shows the soul.
Thy ones note which are thy one's words.
U nbelievable and magical music
Which touches the heart of many.
S axophones, guitars, harps, violins and many
With their rhythm and beats so different and more.
I nstruments inspire the young and make us believe more.
C ontinuous sounds, may we not forget them
And may they stay within people's souls.

Amy Butt (12)
Hilbre High School Humanities College

Bonfire Night

It's Bonfire Night,
Yes it's tonight,
I've waited all day,
I've waited all night.

Fireworks going to great heights,
There are some fantastic sights,
Loud, noisy fireworks,
Orange, red fireworks.

Bang, bang here come the rockets,
We even have twenty-one rockets,
I light the match,
The bonfire lights and goes up.

Bonfire Night is ending soon,
Now there is no moon,
We use up the last few rockets,
And put out the great fire,
What a great night,
This is the best Bonfire Night.

Gregory Roberts (12)
Hilbre High School Humanities College

Dresses

Dresses and skirts
with boob tube too
hot pants and wedges
I love them too

Crop pants and a halter top
go together well
a cute pink bikini and
flip-flops as well

Glitzy dresses and ballgowns
for a posh night out
mini skirt and knee-high boots
tomorrow we hit the town

Cute red braces
which hold up your pants
them sexy flower shoes
with red heart laces

Stripy stilettos and Gucci boots
horrible snake skins
and cute wedges too.

Jess Murray (12)
Hilbre High School Humanities College

My Best Friend

My best friend is always there for me,
She never lets me down,
She's as strong as the ocean sea,
She's really, really sound.

She runs around crazily,
But is as quiet as a bee,
She is really, really caring,
And she hates a cup of tea.

She is smart and funny,
And loves her cat,
Who loves chasing bunnies,
And birds and things like that.

She is a true friend,
Yes she really is,
Our friendship is to the end
My best birthday wish.

Sophie Lloyd (12)
Hilbre High School Humanities College

Rugby

R unning up the pitch having fun,
U nder the blazing sun.
G reat in the very loud crowd,
B ringing great cheers, they're so loud.
Y ou can come, if you can run.

I can run and have fun.
S ound of the crowd is so loud.

G reasby are so easy
R unning makes you smell cheesy.
E verybody running fast,
A t the match you'll never last.
T ries are easy-peasy.

Christopher Wetherall (12)
Hilbre High School Humanities College

Friendship

F riendship means trust to others
R ight or wrongs do not matter.
I n the good times and bad.
E ven when life is sad.
N othing has a stronger power.
D os and don'ts count for nothing.
S outh or east does not matter, distance is nothing.
H atred has no room in this.
I mage is to like, it's what is inside.
P leasing always matters. Friendship means everything.

Elizabeth Hannon (12)
Hilbre High School Humanities College

Marigold

Marigold,
What a funny name,
But whenever someone mentioned it,
There was only me to blame.

I remember those times,
Down at the beach,
Sharing those sweets,
Only 10p each.

I remember her dog,
It wasn't very tame,
We would stand together,
Calling out his name.

As time crept along, soon,
That horrid day came,
And all I have now,
Is her red bloodstain.

Emma Fairbanks (12)
Hilbre High School Humanities College

Best Friends

True friends together,
Best friends forever.
Serious times she's caring
Mad times we're daring.

True friends together,
Best friends forever.
Always together, never apart
If you need us on Saturday we'll be at the park.

True friends together,
Best friends forever.
Sitting doing each other's hair
Loud and crazy but we don't really care.

Sarah-Jayne Edgar-Brown (13)
Hilbre High School Humanities College

My Best Friend Is . . .

My best friend is fun and crazy.
She runs around like a mad daisy
Although she is fun, she never shuts up
Her mouth is as wide as the world's biggest cup.

My best friend is really witty
She is generous and really pretty
She's loving and caring and nuts
And we all say she has a lot of guts.

My best friend has a hamster called Speedy
But sometimes she's just plain greedy.

My best friend is weird in a funny way
She manages to stay in a hype all day.

My best friend is really funny and fab
But when she's angry she looks like a demented crab.

I couldn't ask for a better friend.
Now I'm about to say the end
But I can't say it till I've told you who it is.
It starts with an 's' and ends with an 'e'
I hope you guessed right, it was actually Sophie.

Rebecca Silcock (12)
Hilbre High School Humanities College

Paper Planes

Planes in the air, flying high
Look at that, it can fly!
Things that soar are the best
But ones made of paper, beat the rest.

There are many types to make
But to make one time will take
There are gliders to space age
To really old ones from the ice age.

The best place to test drive a plane
Is class to fry teacher's brain
If your planes are the best
Then it will go and beat all the rest.

Zev Rogan (13)
Hilbre High School Humanities College

My Lil' Powerpuff Girl

My little sister cute and cuddly,
Learning to walk with her pram,
Falling on her bum with a nappy for support,
My little Powerpuff girl is growing up,
I love her lots, I never want to miss her,
She has just turned one and her name is Melissa,
When she grows older, her life's moving on,
She will always be my little sister,
I'll always be sister number one,
Football I'll teach her, to be good on the dance mat too,
She will have lots of friends, maybe even one called Sue,
We'll be friends always, I never want to leave her, sisters always
For ever and ever.

Emma McCabe (12)
Hilbre High School Humanities College

History Lessons

As I hear the bell sounding around school,
I know what comes next.

A history lesson!

We sit down and write the heading,
Another hour of boring dates, people, events.

This is what happens in our history lessons!

What we want to know, never comes our way,
What happened after the battle?
What happened to the bodies?

Did the vultures and birds of prey tear and finish off the bodies?
Ripped, speared, torn, bloody bodies?

We want to know this in our history lessons!

Now the best books on history
Tell us all these things,
The *deaths*, the *blood*, the *wars*
These fabulous books are called

Horrible Histories!

So all you history teachers out there take *no* offence,
All we want really is the *best* history lesson yet!

Aidan Dixon (12)
Hilbre High School Humanities College

School

Walking down the corridor,
Teachers passing by,
'Tuck your shirt in,'
I feel like I'm going to die!

Next lesson is dance,
All the girls are in a trance.
If you don't get enough work done,
You don't get to go on the drum.

Next is break,
I would like a steak,
But a sausage is all,
They have in the hall.

At last the lessons are over today,
I walk home,
But on the way,
It starts to rain, so I can't play.

Will Spicer (12)
Hilbre High School Humanities College

I'm A Girly Girl

I'm a girly girl,
I like shopping, make-up and boys,
I see them as cuddly toys,
I love doing my hair,
My name is cutie Clare

I'm a girly girl,
No football for me,
Got to go home for my tea,
I love to put on jewellery,
It makes me look gorge,

I'm a girly girl,
I'm a girly girl,
I'm a girly girl.

Clare Rohrer (12)
Hilbre High School Humanities College

What Is The Point?

War, is it for love?
Is it for hate?
Is it for revenge? What is it for?

War, is it for land?
Is it for space?
Is it for peace? What is it for?

War, is it for time?
Is it for pride?
What is the point? What is it for?

Sam Holmes (12)
Hilbre High School Humanities College

Friends And Family

Friends and family, they're here for you
Cheering us up and helping us too
Guiding us through the way of life
Teaching us things such as not to play
With a knife.

Bringing us up to a troublesome teenager
Getting us out of trouble, when we're in danger.

So respect them as much as you can.
And they will respect you as a proper man.

Richard Irvine (12)
Hilbre High School Humanities College

Liverpool FC

Liverpool FC are the best,
They are the champions of the north west.
We've got Gonzalez and Riise on the left,
And Pennent sprinting down the right.
Plus Stevie G in the middle,
He'll win any fight.

Our fans are the best in the world,
They'll sing any song known,
Especially 'You'll Never Walk Alone'.
They've helped us win all our cups,
The Champions League, the FA and the UEFA Cup.

Our players they are great,
Super strikers Crouchy and Kuyt.
And the greats from sunny Spain,
Reina, Alonso and Luis Garcia.
Don't forget our rock at the back
Jamie Carragher, he is just the best.

Jack Smith (13)
Hilbre High School Humanities College

Death

As I look at her face.
I wonder should it have been me?
I say my goodbye.
My mum says her goodbye at the prayer stand.
It's raining outside.
I close the coffin.
I weep a bit.
I carry the coffin down the stairs.
I regret putting the coffin in the car.
I close the car door.
And then the sun comes out.
I'll miss her lots.
Goodbye my love.

Oliver Poland (12)
Hilbre High School Humanities College

Holidays

Holidays are a time for sand and sun,
The lifeguard shouts not to run!
I lie on a towel soaking wet,
Looking up at the rising sunset.

On a night when the sun is nigh,
Another day passes by.
I'm having the time of my life,
How can this possibly end?

The minute I step on the plane,
All my memories of England are drained!
There are lots more to come,
When I'm in the sun,
Drinking my day away!

I go swimming off in the pool,
Trying to keep myself cool!
The heat blazes my face . . .
The burns unable to trace!

The tickets are nearly over,
My friends head back to Dover.
It's back on the plane,
Once again . . .
It's back to a 'normal life'.

We'll come back another day,
Maybe next year in the middle of May!
Our stay here was really fun,
Over in England a forbidden sun!

Ryan Harris (12)
Hilbre High School Humanities College

People In The World

There are many different people in the world,
Different colours, religions and race.
And certainly we all look different.
Especially in the face.
But deep down we're all the same.
We all think in the same way.
And the best people in life
Are the people who think with their heart.

Amy Jackson (12)
Hilbre High School Humanities College

Liverpool

L iverpool are the best
I n the League
V ery much better than Madrid
E very player gives their best
R obbie Fowler
P laying football is what they love
O h LFC are the best
O h they have the best fans
L iverpool love the Kop and all the legends.

Elliott Humber (12)
Hilbre High School Humanities College

Pirates' Ships

P irate ship, a disgraceful ship, a rotten ship, an ugly ship
I n a pirate ship the crew lay asleep
R oar the cannons go on the ship's bow
A nd the crew are not a pretty sight
T hey never wash or brush their teeth
E ast and west they sail on the hunt for treasure

S ailing a ship that's what they do
H ave lots of wind to blow the ship through
I n the water deep and blue
P irates sail around the seas
bounty and treasure are their fees.

James Mellors (12)
Hilbre High School Humanities College

Four-Leaved Clover

I look ahead and see everyone dead.
I still can see bombs dropping
And war and everybody sobbing.
I walk past all the smoke then all
Of a sudden someone spoke,
He said, 'Get away while you still can.'
But I couldn't then he ran away.
I cried, 'Wait man!' I ran through all the mist.
I then realised I lost my bracelet off my wrist.
I said to myself, 'I can't wait for this to be over.'
I look down and find a four-leaved clover
Could this be my luck?
I look around and see a truck,
I am saved, I'm back on track,
I wish all the people that died were back.

Rachel Jinkinson & Sammie Hardy (13)
Hilbre High School Humanities College

Dinosaurs

D inosaurs may be tall or may be small,
I n the past they roamed the Earth.
N owhere are they now,
O h! but deep below,
S ome bones still lie.
A nts were huge, talk about big bug problems,
U nder the new world are mysteries yet to be found.
R ound the Earth once they were.
S ome prehistoric monsters lurk in the dark of the sea.

Adam Dore (12)
Hilbre High School Humanities College

Poem About Space

The stars are shining all the time
Night and day come together
It is barren but beautiful
It's huge and endless

Looking back at our origin
The deep blue sea dominant
The land green, brown, grey
There is night and day.

The planets are big and small
Mars is near, Pluto is far
Lifeless but not dead
Unexplored, unresearched, secretive.

Michael Vick (13)
Hilbre High School Humanities College

Daddy

Daddy don't go, Daddy don't leave, please Daddy,
Mummy tell him to stay! Please
I love him, we all love you Daddy.
Things won't be the same without you,
Who's going to read me a bedtime story?
Who's going to wake me up in the morning?
Daddy, Daddy I love you!

Stuart Clegg (13)
Hilbre High School Humanities College

Ryder Cup

R yder Cup
Y oung gun golf makes
D river
E rnie Eels
R obert Rock

C addy
U SA
P utter.

Michael Reynolds (12)
Hilbre High School Humanities College

Horse Riding Today

Round and round, up and down,
Up the hills and round the town,
Trit-trot, tick-tock.
What's the time, check the clock!

Hip hip hooray,
It's time to play,
We can mess around all day,
Now let's feed the horse some hay.

Evening is here,
The horse hears food and pricks his ear,
And now excitement, yes he rears,
And this was the start of the best ever years!

Charlotte Ireland (11)
Hilbre High School Humanities College

Vincent

Vincent Malloy is seven years old,
He's always polite and does what he's told
For a boy his age, he's considerate and nice,
And today he's going to live with Jeffery Price.
He doesn't mind living with his sister, dog and cats,
Now he's going to share a home with spiders, moths and bats.
One night while reading a fairy tale he reads a letter, that made him turn pale.
Such horrible news, he could not survive.
His dad in the war, had been buried alive.
The room started to sway, to shiver and creak,
His horrid insanity had reached its peak.
His memories of his dad being very brave,
He heard him cry from beyond the grave.
He spoke from his coffin and made ghoulish demands,
While through cracking walls, reached skeleton hands.
To escape from the badness he reached for the door.
But he fell limp and lifeless, down on the floor.
His voice was soft and slow,
As he quoted 'The Raven' by Edgar Allan Poe,
And my soul from out that shadow, that he's floating on the floor,
Shall be lifted nevermore.

Suzannah Hamilton (13)
Hilbre High School Humanities College

The Space Captain

Flying through a space odyssey
With complete and utter modesty
The space captain watches the burning sun
Listening to the engine chun,
He goes to capture some fine ships
With his ship called 'The Nips'
On board with his fine crew
With trouble about to brew.
He releases the anchor and jumps
All his crew give the enemy the bumps.

Jordan Clarke-Jones (11)
Hilbre High School Humanities College

Quickster!

Quick!
Fast!
He's always around.
Dodging bullets,
Is like dancing around.
Chasing baddies!
Is as easy as pie.
And he's never,
Ever, ever, ever at the point of time.
Never losing his silver dime,
And the dime will never stop its shine,
It's silver Quickster super shine!

Alastair Moreton (11)
Hilbre High School Humanities College

Space Sailors

Sailing through space, wind in my hair.
I like this feeling, I won't get it anywhere
I see the captain barking his orders.
I want to break out of the mortars.
The sailors load the cannons
While I polish the spears for killing salmons.
I want to go to sleep on my hammock.
And dream all about Saturn's Mammoths.
I want to go home back to Earth,
And warm my feet by the hearth.

Michael Whiting (11)
Hilbre High School Humanities College

The Raw War

The war, the war is so raw
Rations, ration
Soldiers feel the passion.
It all ends up with crashing and bashing,
Then soldiers are dead,
People are not fed,
The country is demolished.
The Germans have been polished,
Hitler committed suicide,
And we won the big collide.

Adam Hashem (11)
Hilbre High School Humanities College

The Flying Nurse

He's quick,
He's fast,
He's sneaky,
Flying through the air,
Up and down and sideways,
Nipping through the air,
Dangling from a long big line,
Saving people's lives.
He's not the usual superhero you're used to
He's my *dad!*

Lewis Pybis (11)
Hilbre High School Humanities College

Shopping

I love to shop,
I shop 'til I drop.
I go with my friend Holly,
She's great fun and so, so jolly
We shop for that,
We shop for this,
We have a laugh trying on a hat
We walk for miles,
We have some lunch,
We always spend our money
But it always makes us smile.

Tanishia Hughes (11)
Hilbre High School Humanities College

Mother Nature

Underground in a secret lair,
She sits,
And knits,
In her flowery wear
I've never seen her but I know what she does.
She waters the flowers and feeds the ground and only because,
She is the saviour of woodland
And sister of spring
Dear Mother Nature what happiness you bring.

Hannah Standing O'Farrell (11)
Hilbre High School Humanities College

My Pirate

Pirates are scary
Pirates are hairy
Pirates are funny
When they've got money

They drink all the rum
And itch their bum
They rob twenty thousand a week
And make the rich weep

The treasure they find
Is worth a few quid
Watch your behind
For here comes the big squid

Yo, ho, ho and away they go.

Alex Mitchell (13)
Hilbre High School Humanities College

Battle On The Open Sea

The sea is choppy and the ship is rocky
Sailing on the open sea
Sailors being cautious in the gunnery
Waiting, waiting, waiting.

Quartermaster at the helm steering the ship with ease
Sailing on the open sea
Crew member in the crow's nest
Watching, watching, watching.

Ship comes alongside, slowly opening the gun shields
Sailing on the open sea
'*Fire!*' says the captain on the deck
Fire, fire, fire!

Mast collapsed onto the deck, hitting the poor captain
Sailing on the open sea
Dead is everyone on this ship
Dead, dead, dead.

Alex Hannah (12)
Hilbre High School Humanities College

Pirates - Captain Bob Blood

Ancient Bob Blood turned his ship round,
and headed for the port
so he could return the note he found
he's not as evil as everyone thought.

The rain, the wind, the snow,
it's all aboard we go,
everyone we know,
because it's all aboard we go.

Sailing overseas,
catching all disease,
Captain Bob Blood is dead,
he must have fallen and cracked his head.

Sorry Bob Blood for your loss,
it was probably for the best
your fave food was candyfloss,
I left some by your grave, I'll leave you to rest.

Kirstie Whitfield (13)
Hilbre High School Humanities College

Pirate's Life

Wind, rain and sea.
Which one will it be?
It'll be all three,
Because it's a pirate's life for me.

Gold treasure
We do it all for pleasure.
To an extreme measure.
Because it's a pirate's life for me.

Holding a sword
We're all aboard
Ready to cheat people into fraud,
Because it's a pirate's life for me.

Lucy Davies (14)
Hilbre High School Humanities College

Pirates

Pirates, pirates
They roam the seven seas
Pirates, pirates
They do whatever they please

They live to loot
Whatever they can find
Always getting the boot
If caught, they face a grind.

Pirates have lots of larks,
Things can change though,
And can be in a nark.
Pirates fear nothing,
Not even a great white shark.

'Aye!
We are ready to go!
And die for our captain if we must
Yo, ho, ho!'

Cameron Borland (13)
Hilbre High School Humanities College

Pirates

He has a long black beard.
He has a patch over his left eye,
His wooden leg knocks on the ground.
His ship has tall black sails.
It is the fastest ship in the world,
It is called the Black Pearl.
His crew are cursed,
When they go into the moonlight they turn to bones . . .

Carl Ames (13)
Hilbre High School Humanities College

Monster From The Deep

100 years ago today,
A sea monster was found
He was big, black, smooth and stinky,
His belly was big and round.
Smooth and silky
He glides through the water
Like silk on a table
The screams and the roars
With his agile claws
Rip through the flesh
With an unwanted death.

Alex Penman (13)
Hilbre High School Humanities College

Pirates

Pirates, they're grubby and stubby
Putrid and stupid
The opposite of Cupid

Pirates, they're not very merry
They're actually kinda scary
With a face and chest
That are really, really hairy

Sailors, they're opposite of wailers
They're really quite posh
And they've got a lot of dosh.

Shipmen, in a way, they're kinda hitmen
Scurvy and curvy
And their minds are topsy-turvy.

Kris Turner (14)
Hilbre High School Humanities College

Pirates Have Fun

The pirate sailed his big black ship
Across the big black sea
He cheered, eating his tea
While drinking a cup of tea.

Stopping sail
While it was hailing
It was too rough
They couldn't handle, it was tough.

It had all stopped
When the engine popped
While they all hopped
The others all mopped.

It all started up and roared,
While all the beer was out and poured
They were off and away
They sailed all the way to Port May.

Fraser Roberts (13)
Hilbre High School Humanities College

Bonfire Night

Sitting round the fire,
the air not very clear,
there are lots of people here,
to help the atmosphere.

It's really burned up high,
Guy Fawkes on the top,
now the fire's going
it's not gonna stop.

The fireworks are set off
flying all around
let's hope no one is hurt
as they come crashing back to the ground.

Kimberley McGeachin (14)
Hilbre High School Humanities College

Pirate's Life

Howl of the wind.
Smell of the sea.
Glow of gold.
Sight from the crow's nest.
Threat of sinking.
Smell of gunpowder.
Sound of clashing swords.
Fire of pistols.
Swig of rum.
Burnt meat.
Stale bread.
I love being a pirate
Down to the depths I go.

Adam Malone (13)
Hilbre High School Humanities College

Pirates

The treasure they steal is for themselves
In their ship there is rum on the shelves
They fight with blades and have monkeys and hats
Some sleep on hammocks, some sleep on mats.

They row their ship across the sea
Making a mark in every town
They are taking stuff, thinking it's free
They steal jewels, gems, diamonds and crowns.

They fill their cannons with balls
When at battle they destroy
To get reinforcement there's a bell that calls
For each battle they have a ploy.

To whoever this is to, we will come to your town.

Jamie Houghton (13)
Hilbre High School Humanities College

Shopping

Pretty pink tops
off-shoulder T-shirts and crops
Shopping's so fun, just shop, shop, shop!

Cute little shoe
Red, white and blue
Shopping's so fun, shop till you drop!

Gorgeous false nails
look so good, you won't fail
Shopping's so fun, shop don't stop!

Najeeda Yasmeen (13)
Hilbre High School Humanities College

Pirates

Pirates are scary
Pirates are hairy
Pirates are funny
Pirates have money

When a pirate gets in battle
He won't shake a bottle
So when a battle commences
The ship condenses
Burn his heart and make him smart

You will remember this as the day
You almost robbed gold
So watch your back
Yo, ho, yo, ho, a pirate's life for me!

Ryan Housley (13)
Hilbre High School Humanities College

Pirates

Pirates are dark.
Pirates are evil.
They are also very lethal
Made their boat out of bark.
So it's tough enough for a shark.
They are not very beautiful.

They dance on the deck
They spill rum on the floor.
So they break their neck.
And ask for more.
Normally the name of the Caribbean captain is Beck.

They get the telescope
Have a look
They find another boat.
Put on our floats.

The bottom of the boat
Is full of gold.
They don't realise it's old.
They get at the gold
They get some ale.

Kieran Watts (13)
Hilbre High School Humanities College

Don't Go

America against Iraq
My dad had to go away
I really didn't want him to
So I wrote this to say.

Daddy I really miss you
Why did you have to do this?
I cry every single night Dad
Waiting for the goodnight kiss.

I miss our fun days out
Now it's just me on my own
I don't know what to do anymore
As I lay here sad and alone.

This is all I have time to say
You will always be in my heart
I'm waiting for the day you return to me
I never thought we would be apart.

Anna Harding-Jones (13)
Hilbre High School Humanities College

I Am A Bully And I Don't Know Why!

I am a bully and I don't know why,
I hit little children and make them cry,
Whenever I go out to play,
All the children run away.

If someone tells me that I am a mutt,
They will be bruised from head to foot.

If they are near me I will skit,
Many children I have hit.

I kick the children down the muddy path,
All my friends can do is laugh.

When I wasn't expecting it the very next day,
The headmaster came to me to say,
I will stop you from always getting your own way!

As he explained how much I hurt the kids,
A tear dribbled from my eyelids.

I tried to be strong but my heart just drained,
So I giggled to try and hide away the pain.

Soon I apologised to keep up my health,
I regret being mean, now I am getting bullied myself.

Sophie Everson (12)
Hilbre High School Humanities College

Friends

My friends are really special to me,
Without them I don't know where I'd be,
When I'm wearing a great big frown,
My friends turn it upside down.

Friends, friends wherever you are,
You're the best friends in the world by far,
Friends, friends what would I do
If the world didn't have you?

I'm never on my own at break,
It's like taking a bite out of a really sweet cake,
We have gallons and gallons of fun,
Everyone's faces are as light as the sun.

Friends, friends wherever you are,
You're the best friends in the world by far,
Friends, friends what would I do,
If the world didn't have you?

Kirsty Rogers (12)
Hilbre High School Humanities College

School

School is a prison,
Just look at the gates,
We work all day,
With hardly any breaks.

Teachers give out detentions and lines,
Like we're all criminals committing a thousand crimes,
You come home from school and feel like a jerk,
You open your bag and you've got loads of work.

All you want to do is sit down and rest,
All school is, a goddamn pest,
The walls are so dull, blue, purple and red,
Have you seen school dinners? No one wants to get fed.

It's all a great laugh when you're with your mates,
When you look over, they're only tiny gates,
At least we have an hour and a bit a day,
Just to sit off and play.

Teachers give merits and treats,
Sometimes we get chocolates and sweets,
We only have thirty minutes of homework a night,
You don't have to be clever or really bright.

School isn't bad at the end of the day,
That's life, just showing you the way.

Harry Hardman (13)
Hilbre High School Humanities College

Pirate Ship

Through the dark black waters the pirate ship sails,
Rippling the calm waters around it,
The skeleton crew work beneath the clear moonlight sky,
Opening the torn black sails.

They prey on defenceless ships,
And they'll destroy the crew,
They'll burn your boat,
And take your loot from you too.

Sailing toward the next victims,
They carve a path in the rough stormy waters,
Lighting the cannons they aim at the ship,
The ship explodes and illuminates the sky.

In calm waters a long way away,
Another innocent crew waits and prays,
They won't be caught by pirates
For another day.

Jane Thornton (13)
Hilbre High School Humanities College

Aaargh!

Yo ho! Yo ho! To the ends of the Earth I'll go!
With my parrot on my shoulder
And my crew who could not be bolder!
Yo ho! Yo ho!

Yee hee? Yee Hee! Oh, the pirate's life is for me!
The skull and crossbones flag a-flying,
We always steal, we're never buying!
Yee hee! Yee hee!

Ya hey! Ya hey! I'm the most swashbuckling pirate today!
You'd better watch out, there's pirates about!
Ya hey! Ya hey!

Oh you'll never get your hands on me booty,
I've hidden it far, far away!
By the time that you have found it,
You'll be in Davy Jones' Locker to stay!

Har har! Har har! We're pirates who've come from afar!
We fill our tums with barrels of rum
Har har! Har har!

Ahoy! Ahoy! We're easy to annoy!
We'll make you walk the plank if you never give us thanks!
Ahoy! Ahoy!

Edward McArdle (13)
Hilbre High School Humanities College

Sweets And Candy

Sweets and candy,
make us happy and dandy,
just like strawberry laces,
delivered in golden cases,
lollipops,
peardrops,
gummy worms,
vanilla squirms,
candy cones,
and chocolate games,
candy lips,
and chocolate pips,
Haribo
how we love them so . . .

Sophie Shepherd (12)
Hilbre High School Humanities College

My Sister Is A Teenager

My sister is a teenager,
She has mood swings now and then.
If she is not in front of the mirror,
She is on MSN.

She has got a huge wardrobe,
But she would rather use the floor.
She tells me to *'Go away!'*
When I knock upon her door.

When she has got boyfriends,
They are always from afar.
This one is from Sweden,
And the next will be from Mars!

She always takes my clothes,
And when I ask for them back.
She has a *huge* hissy fit,
And scratches me like a cat.

Next year I am a teenager,
I really cannot wait.
If I am anything like my sister,
I am someone you will hate!

Sarah Binns (12)
Hilbre High School Humanities College

The Tortured Soul

The pain I feel inside my soul,
Feels like a part of me has been ripped out
And poorly sown back in,
With heartache I walk alone,
I only have the shadows of my deep, dark past.

The only friend I have is a cloud of emotion,
I live in a dark place, known as the world.
The empty streets that feel dead,
I stand alone . . . all alone.

Sat on the kerb in the pouring rain;
I dope over all my past,
Thinking of the loses,
And *no* wins,
All my life I've been deprived from the true world.

I've never seen how people can be happy . . .
As my family was cruel,
They all died with nothing left,
All I have is myself.

I live alone crying myself to sleep every night,
When I wake up, I think this is yet another day,
Another day living through the pain,
I see children playing in the park.

I think to myself . . .
Why couldn't I have this life!
A life of freedom,
A life without caring?

I travel around . . . searching for the one . . .
The one I love,
The one that will never see me,
All my life, she saw right through me,
As if I didn't exist.
Like I wasn't even there.

I want her . . .
But she doesn't even know I exist,
What's the point in living
If the one person I love doesn't know I'm here,
Is there a point?

Joe-Daniel Bennett
Hilbre High School Humanities College

Daddy

Daddy don't go, Daddy don't leave.
Please Daddy!

Mummy tell him to stay please,
I love him
We all love you Daddy

Things won't be the same without you,
Who's going to read me a bedtime story at night?
Who's going to wake me up in the morning?
Daddy, Daddy, Daddy *I love you!*

Ben Banks (13)
Hilbre High School Humanities College

Subjects

All the subjects I am doing are great.
You can really try hard
And have a debate
You feel good doing work
And deciding on what to do.

Business is unique
Or music when you're tapping your feet.
These subjects are a joy
In what you learn and try.

People are annoying
Which makes the teacher angry
Students are worse
As the teacher puts on a dreadful curse.

Really great subjects such as maths
When it is your moment to shine
You do not feel you are doing your SATs.
You get told you have to write lines
Which can be awful at times.
English is a blast
Straight from the dreaded past.
Students write essays
Which makes it difficult for them.

Sport is good to play
When you feel you're in the mood
It can be your day.
If you think it is really fun
As long as you do not complain

Subjects are really interesting
When you can go on trips
You can really learn something.
It is great
When you're not late.

As long as you do well in the subjects
You will learn a lot of things
And now you know what life brings.

Shourjya Chattergee (17)
King George V College

City Life

Dew neatly scattered across a fresh city morning park
Ancient trees huddle close together, cosy in their bark
The early rising joggers trotting past the still and speechless lake
Traffic starts to rumble and the tubes begin to shake

Offices start to fill with drowsy lifeless commuters
Freshly stumbled from their urban city slumbers
They drown in their controlling diversified mass
Of contorted metal and dirty concrete mess

Exorbitant emporiums fling open their crystal encrusted doors
Well-heeled women graze upon the abundant luscious goods
Sitting neatly on the highly-polished floors

The day glides over the city, as people come and go
Wild audiences queue for the slightly cheaper - yet exciting
Matinee show

Haute cuisine becomes the socialising pad under a midday sun
Rich tastes swim together in one aromatic ocean
Sushi, salads, spicy chicken and burgers in a bun

Afternoon simmers slowly onward
When the city starts to boil once more
With the humungous rush to head on homeward
Desperation to get through each unique front door

As the empty belches of the city's motors gradually begin to sigh
The darkness comes to cover them all
Away from the sun's watchful eye

Bright neon lights begin to flicker on
And restaurants serve their best
The chaotic madness has nearly all but gone
And for some it's a well-deserved rest

As we close our eyes to the capital's wondrous strife
We won't forget the torment from this dangerous, poisonous
But beautiful city life.

Alex Whitehill (16)
King George V College

The Pianist

At the touch of her fingers,
The notes will fall like crystal drops,
And gladly, she will linger -
Not to drink in their applause -
But to hear again
The resonating echoes
Of those very last notes.

'Encore!' they cry. 'Encore!'
The wise alone look on and know
That she is but a channel
Through which the lilting music flows;
Touching every listener's heart,
Soothing fears
And calming woes.

She does not make the music:
The music has her in its spell,
Holds her just like her listeners -
Yes, just as well . . .
The wise alone look on and know -
But they won't tell.

Ireti Adejumo (18)
King George V College

Committed To The Memory Of War

The fear of that night does still ensue occasionally within my heart,
The chill of shrieks from the blood-choked lungs as they take their
last breath.
The cause: a satanic bolt from the barrel of a Hell-stricken demon,
Taken to the air by a tap of anguish, created by a country of one.

The hammer of barrage still rings in the ear as if it were yesterday.
The taking of another's life, for the good of the bad of existence.
The lives of so many placed on the altar for a petty regime corrupt
on expansion.
Expansion not worth the loss of so many, and the gain of so few.

Jonathan Fleming (16)
Liverpool College

Young Writers Information

We hope you have enjoyed reading this book - and that you will continue to enjoy it in the coming years.

If you like reading and writing poetry drop us a line, or give us a call, and we'll send you a free information pack.

Alternatively if you would like to order further copies of this book or any of our other titles, then please give us a call or log onto our website at www.youngwriters.co.uk

Young Writers Information
Remus House
Coltsfoot Drive
Peterborough
PE2 9JX

(01733) 890066